Building Wealth through Real Estate Investing

Coach Dr JAG Guide to Investing and Recurring Income in Real Estate

Coach Dr. JAG

LifeMAPS Consulting

Disclaimer 1

The investment strategy that will be expressed, described, and explained in this short book is not failsafe or fool proof. As in any investment there is potential risk. Please consult with experts in the field as to your area and what is a sound investment. These are ideas and suggestions that of been proven to be successful. The results may not be the same for you as they have been for others. There is a potential for loss as well as a greater potential for massive games utilizing the right strategy that is right for you as an individual.   Many have made a business out of this and been able to replace their current profession. Others have developed a significant income portfolio that divests and I versifies investment tools for an ever-changing economy.

Disclaimer 2

The numbers shared in this book are a representation of the concept and proposed plan being presented. Results will vary by individual and circumstances. The author cannot guarantee these results. Please consult a licensed financial, legal, and real estate investing professional in good standing in your area before moving forward on this plan or any investing plan. A minor fee may be required by these professional, though they can provide critical information, representation, and peace of mind rather than going it alone, uninformed or unprepared.

Disclaimer 3

The book has been reviewed, read, re-read, and edited over multiple iterations. It is possible there are grammatical, spelling, and syntax errors. Considerable effort has been made to reduce or remove these errors. Please excuse these errors should you come across one. Our sincere apologies in advance should one occur. Please consider the content over the error if possible. If you would kindly drop me a line at jonathan@lifemapsonline.net indicating the error, how it should read, along with the page number and paragraph number as the error can then be corrected in a future updated edition. The more eyes, the more likely to make a near perfect copy. Thank you in advance.

Coach Dr JAG Guide to Starting to Invest in Real Estate 2016©

Contents

Introduction

Is it possible that we will try to invest but we will feel overwhelmed by the need for liquid cash assets that we tend to forget what the long-term advantage can be? We often tend to move away from sound investing practices in favor of short-term cash liquidation. What if there was a way to invest in more long-term investment tools without necessarily risking greater cash flow issues? What if we could find a way to make our money work for us? Could we use it while increasing our rate of return for a greater investment? That is the purpose of this book.

The models that we are going to use are an example. You may have to look around and see what is viable in your community or surrounding areas. If you are in a high property value area such as certain parts in the western portions of Southern California or the San Francisco Bay area. You could be in New York, or Washington DC these tend to be very expensive areas to live. Look around as to what is within a reasonable distance for you as to what might be more affordable in order to get you started.

You may choose to live in one of these investment homes. If you are only looking at investment properties for renting to others, remember you are not buying for you to live in. The home does not have to be perfect for you to live in. It takes all types that have differing needs. You are purchasing rental incomes not personal residence. Buying homes below market value and flipping them after maximizing potential is also a terrific opportunity if done right. Such investing is not in the immediate scope of this book. Flipping homes is the topic of another book to come at a later date.

If you live in a less expensive property value area you may be able to start at a lower rate or make a different investment strategy. There is also a possibility that you may need to team up with others to keep any additional investment low. Explore the possibilities available to you. Often times resources are right in front of us every day and we do not see them as they are so regularly available to us. Multiple investors may keep investment low financially while cost is more in other areas through the partnership or alliance. There would need to be a consensus in that respect as well as a well written contract in case of unforeseen circumstances.

The contents of this short book is a potential strategy that will lay out some key ideas. It is not considered professional advice. The author is not a licensed real estate agent or broker. Please consult a licensed professional in your area that also understands the real estate values in your area and the laws in your state or region. It is recommended you find someone that knows the rental market and how to spot a deal, working with you to get a better opportunity. Often there are real estate and legal professionals in your area that specialize in this type of investing as there are also real estate investment groups or funds. If you use a real estate agent, it is strongly recommended you use a licensed and accredited Realtor®. The Realtor® symbol is a sign of quality and integrity. Not all agents are accredited.

The Experiment

At age 20 years old you have saved up $5000. This is a sizable amount of money in which you would like to invest. Many of your friends might suggest that you use that for a vacation or to put towards a new vehicle. If you would like to see a greater return on the money consider some other alternatives. You could put this money on the counter or use stock investments. You could also use this as a down payment on a small house or condominium. Depending on your circumstances and situation, it is time to consider an investment strategy. What is it that you want to accomplish? At 20 years old we often are not thinking about retirement, though we truly should investigate the options we make at 20 and consistently thereafter will have profound impact on our financial condition at 50, 60, and 70, or 80 and above.

An individual that invests $5000 at 20 years old in an investment tool earning on average 10% per annum, and continues to add approximately $3600 a year or $300 per month every month will have over $1 million of the time they are 55 years old. If they continue to increase the investment amount by 10% of their investment amount with gradually increasing amount going up by 10% every year the point to reach a $1,000,000 goal will be significantly shortened.

Here's the clincher, every seven years after the initial investment period the money will double if you continue the pattern of duplicating behavior. That means by age 62 there is 2 Million on the account, my age 69 there is over 4 million, and my age 76 when most people have to seriously consider retirement you will have over $8 million in investment revenue before taxes. At that point you can live on 10% or less and not have to touch the principal. Most likely you can live on far less, even with taxes, and continue to invest even though you may not be contributing income anymore. Individuals that work in real estate have often been very successful for solid investing practices. While this book is a start continue to study your craft. Read the books on the topic. Speak with others that are doing the same and are successful. Find a mentor that is doing this and a few steps ahead of you. Become the best in what you do.

However you must be an informed and knowledgeable investor with the right resources that you are willing to develop. Consider the table below as to an investment time table using other methods than real estate.

How long will it take?						
Daily ($)	Month ($)	ROI %	Years to 1M	Years to 2M	Years to 3 M	Years to 5 M
0.01	0.3	10	108	100+	100+	100+
0.03	1	10	91	98	100+	100+
1	30	10	57	64	68	73
2	60	10	50	57	61	66
5	150	10	41	48	52	57
10	300	10	34	41	45	50
20	600	10	28	34	38	42
33	1000	10	23	29	33	38
65	2000	10	17	23	26	31

The other option, the whole $5000 can be used for purchasing a lease to own option a lower priced house or condominium that is priced at around $30-$40,000. Depending on the environment and financing available as well as your financial condition you may be able to qualify for special financing requiring a lesser down payment as well as possible financial assistance and federal assistance in order to renovate the area or you provide housing to the indigent or low socioeconomic (There are programs that can aid you, such as grants, and government aid, lowering your personal cash investment).

You can also choose to live in this house or residence, possibly lowering your outlay for living and investing. You may choose to purchase a house that is in need of repair. A distressed property is the reason for a very good price on it. You can live in it while making the repairs. The money you would spend on rent is now going towards the payment of this income property. The money is beginning to work for you. If you spend $500 a month on a one bedroom apartment. And you have bought a $40,000 condominium it is not costing you $500 a month anymore in rent. It should be costing you a little bit less and you can put some of that money towards repairs and fixing it up. If you purchase right there are tax advantages as well (please consult a tax professional for the laws in your area). You can add the amount to the principal and pay down the mortgage that much faster. Remember this may not be your dream home, in fact it likely is not, though you are taking steps towards what you are seeking.

We will talk more about these ideas later in the book. The key is to begin a strategy as to what you are willing to pay. Where can you start and what do you need to do? You may need to build up enough cash to make the initial investment in real estate. There are ways to do this to build money more rapidly as well as looking at ways to develop capital resources for revenue building can include options, including a part-time job, cutting expenses, or selling items you are not using but storing, or creating a second source of income, consulting making a product, or delivering a service. For more information on these processes, consider other Coach Dr JAG books on the chosen topic. The books serve as a guide to start you for t on the path.

Sidebar: CoachDrJAG books serve as a user friendly guide to consider these topics. There are different ways to gather information or learn a process. We can invest time and resources to learn this on our own. We can learn from others. We can hire someone to teach us. We can hire someone to complete the research for us. If you were to hire a researcher this could cost you hundreds if not thousands of dollars. You could hire a consultant to research and teach these processes (the author's fee for this is in the hundreds of dollars per hour). Or, you find resources that have done the research and explained the processes for you through books, periodicals, newsletters, blogs, and videos. These are usually more readily available to cater to your schedule and fit most everyone's budget. It is said if you wanted to consult with an expert in the real estate field, doing some of the things we are discussing that are highly successful such as a Donald Trump or Robert Kiyosaki, even Robert Allen or Carlton Sheets, they would charge thousands if not tens of thousands per hour. Each of these experts though have made a system available for a much more reasonable price to get you started. If you continue to advance, you can them increase your level of service and pay more because you are making more. The book you are holding if in hardcopy is a few dollars. If you are reading an electronic copy it was likely less. These resources are available to you when you are ready and as you are ready on your time at your pace. It is very easy, but you must start. START where you are at, not where you perceive yourself to be!

It is important to continually consider your options and opportunities. Keep a watchful eye out on opportunities that may allow you to significantly increase or improve your standing. You will never be aware if an opportunity looks too good, unless you ask questions or find someone who knows the right questions to ask as well as possibly maybe a trap somewhere in the deal. There are risks that may be undertaken that are reasonable understand conditions, though unacceptable under very different circumstances. A few minor adjustments to make the difference between a tremendous deal, and a tumultuous deal. Know what is being offered. Know what you can do and what you're willing to except ass reasonable risk for a reasonable return. I cannot emphasize this enough.

Shortly, I will show you a 20 year plan that will result as follows:
- 2 homes purchased at 40K 20 years ago, paid off (Minimum value is 80K).
- 1 home at 100K 16 years ago, paid off. (Minimum value is 100K).
- 4 homes purchased at 100K 13-15 years ago, paid off (Minimum Value is 400K).
- 3 homes purchased at 150K 11-12 years ago, paid off (Minimum value is 450K).
- 8 homes (averaged) purchased at 120K 5-10 years ago, owe less than 60K per property (480K total debt) (Equity Minimum 480K).
- 15 homes purchased at 150K 0-5 years ago, Owe 100K per property (average) or (1.5 Million in debt). (Minimum Equity 750K).
- You will have mortgages of just under 2 Million dollars.
- Equity of $2,260,000, or you have assets above liabilities of over $300,000 if all debt was settled.
- In paper you have a real estate portfolio worth in excess of 4.24 Million dollars acquired in just 20 years.

*The reality is in many U.S. and global markets the properties have continued to climb in value over the life of you ownership. The homes you purchased 20 years ago may have nearly doubled in value or more. There is no guarantee of such results.

A home built in CA in 1969 for 28,000 in 2009 was valued at over 650,000. This was not in one of the high home price areas of CA but a more moderately priced area. In 1995 a home was purchased just north of Los Angeles County for 110,000. The same house sold for 170,000 in 2002 just seven years later. These are not exceptional deals or extraordinary homes. They were purchased smart. Using these examples the potential for the above example could value the portfolio at over 5 Million dollars with ever increasing value. Remember like any market though corrections occur thus so does the value and available equity in the investment portfolio. A few tweaks can mean the difference between exceptional profits and being upside down, owing more than the property is worth.

Home investing plan 1:

Initial startup capital $ 2500
Monthly payments 400
Monthly payments above minimum 100

Purchase a property in the $30-50,000 range (likely 2 bedroom condo or house in need of repairs)
Use the $2,000 to initiate a lease to own arrangement, first month, last month, security deposit.
This will likely be a private deal between current owner and purchaser (you). Research a sound contract or legal service to insure all pertinent areas are addressed (Title, payments, duration, forfeiture of funds, responsibilities of parties, insurance, and maintenance, etc.) Peripheral services can be retained for reasonable prices if we shop smart.

If you choose to live in this property, what you would pay for rent will now be going towards development of equity in the property.

The remaining $500 can go to legal fees and basic clean-up of property to start.
You might consider a low cost legal service, such as prepaid legal or legalzoom.com in order to keep legal costs manageable.

Agree on a monthly payment and how much each month will go to principal. The immediate goal is to have a minimum of 20% equity in the property and a solid payment record for a minimum 6 months, 2 years is better.

If lease payment on a $40,000 property is 400 per month. Consider payment options of:
Pay 200/biweekly
Pay 200/2x per month
Pay 400 1x per month

Options 1 & 2 will assist in paying down the debt faster. Paying $200 bi-weekly means 26 payments per year instead of 12 monthly payments. You pay more though if your pay is bi-weekly it is an automatic payment that comes out of every paycheck. This process will make an extra monthly payment every year, and interest is not accruing as fast due to the more frequent payments. Over a ten year period this could save a few thousand dollars in interest that can be applied to other properties. Option three is viable and consistent. You will still be accruing equity though slower. You may need to start here, though consider moving to the 2x per month plan, then the bi weekly over a designated time frame. The difference can be significant and the motivation as you see the loan amount reducing is encouraging.

General Action Plan, Phase 1 (5 years)

Year 1

Property 1: 30-50,000
Initial Investment 2500-10,000*
Rent: 600
Required mortgage payment: 400/mo.
Add. Payment 100*/mo.
Income:
- Payment $100-goes to capital fund (repairs, upgrade, down payment towards next prop)
- From paid income (Job) feed $100/mo. into the capital account.
- The $100 is deposited regularly, earmarked for repairs or down payment for next prop.

Year 2

Property 1 paying 7200/year revenue on 30K loan.
- Tenant shift increase rent 5-10% dep on mkt.
- It is better to keep rent the same longer with a good tenant than to continually change tenants.
Paid: 4800 on 30K loan for 35-40K property.
    With an extra $100 payment per month, paid almost 6000 on the loan and interest.
Income account save any repairs (should have over 1K in it)
    (Build safety net account, keep costs down w/o being hit by surprise expenses)
Goal: increase contribution by property and personal income by 10%**
Savings goal by End of Year /EOY, Goal is $2500-4000 in the capital account.

Year 3

Property 1
- Should be self-sufficient and generating a small profit while paying additional on the loan to pay down faster.
- Increase rent to what similar properties in market will bear. Even with established tenant raise the rent 5-10% (every 24 months is not outrageous).

By mid-year:
Purchase property 2.
- 40-50K property (Buy Smart).
- 50K property will need to generate approximately 600-750/mo. income.

Payment 500/mo.
Additional Pmt. 100/mo.
Pay capital fund from property 100/mo.
Personal income contribution 100/mo.
Within 2 years of this purchase, the property should be producing near 1K/mo. revenue before expenses.

Year 4

Property 1 Self-sustaining. Make necessary repairs, minor improvements.
- Increase payments by 100/mo. to principal.
- Increase payments to capital fund by 100/mo.

Property 2 Mostly self-sustaining save any major repairs.
- Maintain the path looking for minor adjustments to lower overhead or increase income.
- Do not compromise integrity.
- Follow the rent increase plan of Prop 1 if sustainable (market bearable).
- Continually build the safety net and down payment fund.

Purchase Property 3. Look for the right mix of:
- Size (maybe a 3Br 2 Ba).
- Location (Schools, Businesses, Downtown, or Shopping).
- Property should be in 75-100K range.
- Rent collected should be 1000-1500/month.
- Look for opportunities to buy right and buy smart. (Distressed, credit problem, foreclosure).
- Follow the same steps as to paying above the required minimum.
- Pay the capital account monthly regularly (automatic) without thought or question. (consider direct deposit, if possible)
- Pay the capital account from personal income regularly without thought or question.

Year 5

Let's take a moment to review
Property 1 was purchased for 40K, 60 months ago.
- Paid a $5,000 down payment towards price of property leaving a $35,000 Note.
- You have paid 500/mo. for 36 months (18K) and 600/mo. for 12 months (7200) for a total of $30,200.
- Interest at around 10% (mkt) on the decreasing amount will be around 11K.
- $22,000 remaining on the loan continuing to accrue interest.
- Rent is now around 750/m.
- Could refinance payoff the loan, get a lower interest rate or monthly payment
- Consider options allowing for greater revenue income to be put into the capital fund.
- ***Build that fund!***

Property 2 Purchased 40K, 42 months ago.
- $5,000 down payment towards price of property leaving a $35,000 Note.
- You have paid 500/mo. for 36 months (18K) and 600/mo.
- $26,600 based on 6 months (3600 +18000+ 5,000).
- Interest accrued will be around $9,000 at 10%.

- Equity will be 16,000 and change.
- Rent 700-750/mo. if market allows.

Okay. Let's take a closer look.

It is possible if you have maintained a clean credit rating you can qualify for loans of 5% or less and a mortgage of around 200/mo. on a 30 year loan for $25,000. Potentially placing about 500/mo. in the coffers each for properties 1 & 2 for a total of about $1000 per month. This is in addition to the progressive personal income you are regularly contributing. If the plan is firing on all cylinders should be a total of around 1300-1500/month after mortgage payments.

The capital fund should be growing. It is advisable to keep around $15,000 liquid for immediate repairs or a quick purchase if the offer requires immediate action. Rebuild to a minimum of 10K as soon as possible or at least a 10K credit line.

The purchase of property 3 at $100,000 will give you around $200,000 in properties on paper. Granted these are heavily leveraged at this time. In five years though you have established a solid system for generating income. By learning to develop a solid system and looking for deals, developing contacts and refining your contracts, you are producing a tidy side income to start. If you have not by this point, it is time to determine how much is needed to make in order to achieve the passive income you want. Hopefully you have done this before you purchased the first property. Ideally you will review this plan at least annually to determine progress and if modification is necessary.

If you do nothing else other than maintaining these properties from here on out making improvements as needed Properties 1 and 2 can be paid off in an additional 20 years on a low interest loan, while acquiring a substantial monthly income. Consider the advantages and disadvantages of paying off a property quickly or slowly. Check with a financial and tax expert as to a sound method that aligns with your goals. Sooner debt retirement means larger income sooner rather than later.

The third property can be paid for comfortably in 25 years while enjoying a moderate income. In 25 years from now or 30 years from when you started you would likely own 3 properties that have at least doubled in value depending on where you bought and how you maintained them. This is where buying smart can pay massive dividends. The 3 properties could be worth in the neighborhood of $400,000 30 years from original purchase. The income from these properties should have literally tripled from the original purchase price and rent paid then If rent for the 2 $40,000 properties were 500/mo. to start, in 30 years 1500-2000 is not unreasonable as the market will bear this. The combined income would be $3,000/mo. for Properties 1 & 2. The two properties are paid off, thus other than maintenance, the income is yours after paying the taxes and property management fees, should you use a manager.

Property 3 would be approximately another $3000 per month while the mortgage has been retired. The property are paid for. You are in maintenance mode. This all sounds good. The reality is though that yes 6K/mo. is nice but it is in the dollar amounts of 30 years from start thus 6000 in 2016 looks very different than 6000/mo. in 2046.

The plan to this point has been the very foundation in which to start. It is not uncommon for real estate investors seeking to solidify and develop their portfolios will continue to build up their properties and branch out as to what they purchase. More often than not they will stay within a niche market (location, type of property) as they stay with their strategy that is proven. You could choose to stop here and already have a consistent $60,000 annual retirement in real estate alone in 25 years, starting at age 45. If you were to continue depending on your plans, the potential and momentum is still gaining traction, with that in mind let's return to Phase 2 of the plan.

General Action Plan, Phase 2 (5 years).

Year 6

Pay down on Properties 1-3 by an additional 20-30% in payments. By so doing payoff will be approximately 10 years for the life of the original loan. By year 10 these properties are paid off, free and clear, except taxes, and maintenance. Debt reduction this year will result in substantial savings as to payment to principal and interest savings, as well as early debt retirement.

Years 7-10

Focus on purchasing in the chosen market (2 BR condo, or 3/2 house), these are sometimes called bread and butter homes by investors as they are very common and quite affordable. Many are required for most living situations. Depending on market purchase for around 100-150,000. Some areas are considerably more expensive. The goal to purchase an addition 3/2 each year during this time. The result gives you 5 Bread and Butter properties in addition to the initial 2 starter properties. Focus on paying these properties down, though more on buying smart by location and style of property. Become the expert in the area on this type of property and look for these deals. Become a problem solver with a cash account to make the better deals that those without cash cannot make.

Years 9-10 Purchase 3 more properties in the bread and butter segment or 2 slightly higher priced 150-200,000 segment in the 3/2 or 4/3 arena if buying smart. The initial positive cash flow will be minimal though the original properties should help to offset temporary setbacks. It is common that a property takes 24-36 months to show a significant profit. By now you own multiple properties and have developed your own systems and resources to maintain costs and minimize overhead where possible.

Remember to reinvest the income from the properties back into the properties or acquiring more properties. By reinvesting you will grow the portfolio exponentially faster than if you begin drawing significant sums early to support lifestyle. A $2,000 "borrow" from the account at age 25 without restoring the money with interest will cost around 40,000 by age 45 and over $80,000 by age 65. Small decisions made consistently will greatly impact over the long term.

Year 10 goal:

Properties 1-3 paid off. Anticipated value $200,000. Loans are retired. If you chose to refinance to a low interest loan, the difference in payment is being reinvested.

Properties 4-6 should be nearing around the 50% paid off leaving an approximate average loan value of 50-75K per property. The remainder of these loans is around 200-225K. Rent earned before expenses should be around 4500 per month collectively. Combined with the $2000 per month from the paid off properties (1-3), brings earning to around $6500/mo. before expenses. Properties 7-9 are still fairly high on the debt counter, though are gradually coming down. These mortgages are another $200-300,000 in mortgages, though collecting 4500-5000/mo. before expenses.

Let's look at the plan closer.

Rent collected is 4500+2,000+4500= $11,000 per month with mortgages of around 5500-6000 per month which you are working on paying down. The amount is $11,000 on paper, not in reality. You are continuing to contribute a portion of your retirement planning/investing dollars out of every paycheck (can be done pretax to lower your tax bill) Now this sounds great, though there is the likelihood of major repairs, tax bills, or vacancies. So planning on an extra $5,000 every month sounds terrific though likely is not a reality. As stated earlier in the plan, you have been building up the nest egg in case of disaster such as major repairs like painting, a new roof, a new driveway.

The next several years is where this can get to be a lot of fun for those that will commit.

Years 11-15 Phase 3

Earmark $3500 of the $5000 each month for capital to purchase another property. Doing this is addition to your investing money (70% of this is earmarked for capital as well).

Purchase a property (100-120K) on average every 9 months (20-30% down, buying smart), for a total 6 more properties. If you went 20% down and bought every 6 months, you would acquire potentially 10 more properties, though profit per property would be less, the total number of homes can assist in offsetting the vacant properties or the repairs.

Years 16-20 Phase 4

Earmark funds of 5K/per month from net revenues, this plus 70% of investment money should be in excess of 6500/mo. Four months at 6500 each is 26,000 for down payment.

Purchase 3 properties per year at 125-150K per year. By year 20, you will have purchased another 15 homes. You may say this is an aggressive plan, and it is. The plan is totally workable if you will commit to the plan. The timelines used in this book is a guideline. Depending on your willingness to risk and commitment will assist in determining a timeline for the strategic action plan. Adjust the plan to your specific needs, though commit to what you can and will do, then stay faithful to this plan, even in adversity or in times of plenty.

We talk about different options for funding and an actual timeline the Coach Dr JAG books, though this book is more as to how to start a real estate investing portfolio. There are many variables in play. By the end of year 20, you will own 30 properties based on the conservative side and 34 homes on the more risky side.

The 20 Year Plan Summary

- 2 homes purchased at 40K 20 years ago, paid off (Minimum value is 80K).
- 1 home at 100K 16 years ago, paid off. (Minimum value is 100K).
- 4 homes purchased at 100K 13-15 years ago, paid off (Minimum Value is 400K).
- 3 homes purchased at 150K 11-12 years ago, paid off (Minimum value is 450K).
- 8 homes (averaged) purchased at 120K 5-10 years ago, owe less than 60K per property (480K total debt) (Equity Minimum 480K).
- 15 homes purchased at 150K 0-5 years ago, Owe 100K per property (average) or (1.5 Million in debt). (Minimum Equity 750K).

You will have mortgages of just under 2 Million dollars. Yes this sounds high, though read on.

- You have Equity of $2,260,000.
- You have assets above liabilities of over $300,000 if all debt was settled.
- The real estate portfolio on paper is worth in excess of 4.24 Million dollars acquired in just 20 years.
- You are 40 years old (because you started small at 20 but were committed).
    - Consider if you used this as a foundation for another 20 year plan.
    - Teach someone else to do the same as you have done, mentor and guide.
    - Be a resource to others.
    - Be the best in your area.
    - Be willing to learn.

The reality is in most markets the properties have continued to increase the value over the life of ownership. The homes you purchased 20 years ago may have nearly doubled in value or more.

It is easy to want to go beyond the scope of this book.

There are so many components that are necessary in order to make investing in real estate lucrative. It is important to do your homework and be well informed. Please do not let this book be you're only resource. It is important to have a large cross-section of knowledge in order to make an informed decision. This book is not legal advice, financial advice, or given by a licensed real estate agent in any given state. The information offered is through research, investigation, interview, and study.

Take the information provided as a tool, then go and sharpen your tools in gaining the work tools to put in your toolbox. Be more effective using the right tool for the right purpose. This is more for informational purposes then for straight investing without the guidance of a licensed professional. Seek a licensed professional in your area that knows the area as well as the ins and outs of the market in your area. There are Realtors® that specialize in investing, property management, and flipping houses.

The models that are demonstrated in this book are all slightly different. There is no one set model that works in all situations. Use these models as a guideline. Some people will invest more. Others will not invest as much. Some investors will make a plan for 10 years. Still others will make a plan for 30 or 40 years and build it into either a strong supplemental income or replace the current income and expand into other areas. Whatever your choice, please use this as an inspiration and a guide as to what is possible. This is not to be substituted though for sound financial counseling from a licensed professional in your area in this given field.

Closing thoughts.

Be a problem solver. Do not create more problems for a buyer, seller, lender, or renter. If you can solve their problem, it becomes a win -win situation for everybody. You also become the go to person which tends to open up greater opportunities all the way around and can save a lot of time, energy, resources, and money.

If you believe you do not have the resources to start investing, take a serious look at your budget and determine what you can do even if it means sacrificial giving for a few years. The process may include giving up certain luxuries that may seem like necessities.

If necessary look at developing investment partners that you split the costs or develop an amicable agreement. It is strongly suggested that if you do this develop a contract upfront as to what each party's role is as well as what is expected in the way of investing as well as what is expected in the way of returns and sharing of profit. Partnerships can be a blessing or a horrible idea. Often it is and how they are set up initially they can make such a difference should the partnership need to be dissolved.

Think proactively. Do not just go on a handshake and each other's word. Have a solid written contract that is legal. Seek legal counsel as to how to do this and what needs to be included. The key is to start somewhere even if it takes five years to get the down payment for the first house. Develop a plan you can do and get started. Take massive action!

Become an educated investor it is important to develop the right attitude and behavior of studying, and consistently taking action. Talk will not get the job done that is only one variable of the complete package. Action is required.

The models used speak of purchasing homes in the $40-$60,000 range as well after $70-$100,000 range. These are not high end properties. These are simple low end homes that you will put some money into but you're not expected to maintain a high quality but medium living. Fixtures and repairs should be at a minimum. Do not skimp, but be reasonable as to what you put in. Sometimes the cheapest is not the best option. Make it nice. You may be able to get a little additional rent or maintain your tenants a little bit longer which lowers overhead and turnover of tenants.

Develop a strategy that works for you and your investment plan. It is understood the different areas will have different price points. This is why you must work with someone who is licensed and highly qualified in your area. It may cost you something.

Develop that relationship. You may also negotiate their commission by giving them part ownership in the property. They may also be in investing partner. Be creative in how you address financial needs.

Financial needs does not always mean cash on the barrelhead. You may be able to develop other options or opportunities that delay paying out a cash settlement. You may be able to provide something of value that will save you money and time in the long run. Look for these alternatives. Find out what is truly needed. Money is not always the need. Be open to options and alternatives.

Sometimes you can get the property by taking over payments with a minimum cash down payment. You also may be able to structure something with the lender to take over the loan. You may be able to keep the owner in the house as a tenant paying you rent and you resettle the loan at a lower rate to put some money in your pocket. These are all options however this is a different book altogether.

Remember…

Know what you know

Know what you do not know

Learn what you do not know so you know.

Know so that you know

To you Wealth!!

Sample Template/Worksheet.
Plug in the numbers that work for you. A guide has been provided.

Year 1	$/mo. cap fund		Year 1	$/mo. cap fund	Salary: 50K
Mo 1			Mo 1	417	4167
Mo 2			Mo 2	417	4167
Mo 3			Mo 3	417	4167
Mo 4			Mo 4	417	4167
Mo 5			Mo 5	417	4167
Mo 6			Mo 6	417	4167
Mo 7			Mo 7	417	4167
Mo 8			Mo 8	417	4167
Mo 9			Mo 9	417	4167
Mo10			Mo10	417	4167
Mo11			Mo11	417	4167
Mo12			Mo12	417	4167
			Total	**5004**	**50004**
Purchase			Purchase	40000	
Property			Property	1	
Down			Down	5000	
Payment			Payment	400	
Income			*Income*	*100*	

Year 2	$/mo. cap fund		Year 2	$/mo. cap fund	52000 (4%raise)
			Mo 1		
Mo 1			(11%)	477	4333
Mo 2			Mo 2	477	4333
Mo 3			Mo 3	477	4333
Mo 4			Mo 4	477	4333
Mo 5			Mo 5	477	4333
Mo 6			Mo 6	477	4333
Mo 7			Mo 7	477	4333
Mo 8			Mo 8	477	4333
Mo 9			Mo 9	477	4333
Mo10			Mo10	477	4333
Mo11			Mo11	477	4333
Mo12			Mo12	477	4333
			Total	**5724**	**51996**
Purchase			Purchase	40000	
Property			Property	2	
Down			Down	5500	
Payment			Payment	400	
Income			*Income*	*100*	

Year 3	$/mo. cap fund	Year 3	$/mo. cap fund	55000
Mo 1		Mo 1 (12%)	550	4583
Mo 2		Mo 2	550	4583
Mo 3		Mo 3	550	4583
Mo 4		Mo 4	550	4583
Mo 5		Mo 5	550	4583
Mo 6		Mo 6	550	4583
Mo 7		Mo 7	550	4583
Mo 8		Mo 8	550	4583
Mo 9		Mo 9	550	4583
Mo10		Mo10	550	4583
Mo11		Mo11	550	4583
Mo12		Mo12	550	4583
		Total	**6600**	**54996**
Purchase		Purchase	40000	
Property		Property	3	
Down		Down	6000	
Payment		Payment	400	
Income		*Income*	*100*	

Year 4	$/mo. cap fund	Year 4	$/mo. cap fund	57750
Mo 1		Mo 1 (14%)	674	4813
Mo 2		Mo 2	674	4813
Mo 3		Mo 3	674	4813
Mo 4		Mo 4	674	4813
Mo 5		Mo 5	674	4813
Mo 6		Mo 6	674	4813
Mo 7		Mo 7	674	4813
Mo 8		Mo 8	674	4813
Mo 9		Mo 9	674	4813
Mo10		Mo10	674	4813
Mo11		Mo11	674	4813
Mo12		Mo12	674	4813
		Total	**8088**	**57756**
Purchase		Purchase	40000 (2)	
Property		Property	4,5	
Down		Down	5000	
Payment		Payment	500	
Income		*Income*	*200*	

Year 5	$/mo. cap fund	Year 5	$/mo. cap fund	60637
Mo 1		Mo 1 (16%)	808	5053
Mo 2		Mo 2	808	5053
Mo 3		Mo 3	808	5053
Mo 4		Mo 4	808	5053
Mo 5		Mo 5	808	5053
Mo 6		Mo 6	808	5053
Mo 7		Mo 7	808	5053
Mo 8		Mo 8	808	5053
Mo 9		Mo 9	808	5053
Mo10		Mo10	808	5053
Mo11		Mo11	808	5053
Mo12		Mo12	808	5053
		Total	**9696**	**60636**
Purchase		Purchase	75000	
Property		Property	6	
Down		Down	9500	
Payment		Payment	800	
Income		*Income*	*200*	

Year 6	$/mo. cap fund	Year 6	$/mo. cap fund	70000
Mo 1		Mo 1 (18%)	1050	5833
Mo 2		Mo 2	1050	5833
Mo 3		Mo 3	1050	5833
Mo 4		Mo 4	1050	5833
Mo 5		Mo 5	1050	5833
Mo 6		Mo 6	1050	5833
Mo 7		Mo 7	1050	5833
Mo 8		Mo 8	1050	5833
Mo 9		Mo 9	1050	5833
Mo10		Mo10	1050	5833
Mo11		Mo11	1050	5833
Mo12		Mo12	1050	5833
		Total	**12600**	**69996**
Purchase		Purchase	40000 (2)	
Property		Property	7,8	
Down		Down	12,000	
Payment		Payment	800	
Income		*Income*	*250*	

Year 7	$/mo. cap fund	Year 7	$/mo. cap fund	73500
Mo 1		Mo 1 (20%)	1225	6125
Mo 2		Mo 2	1225	6125
Mo 3		Mo 3	1225	6125
Mo 4		Mo 4	1225	6125
Mo 5		Mo 5	1225	6125
Mo 6		Mo 6	1225	6125
Mo 7		Mo 7	1225	6125
Mo 8		Mo 8	1225	6125
Mo 9		Mo 9	1225	6125
Mo10		Mo10	1225	6125
Mo11		Mo11	1225	6125
Mo12		Mo12	1225	6125
		Total	**14700**	**73500**
Purchase		Purchase	50000 (2)	
Property		Property	9, 10	
Down		Down	14000	
Payment		Payment	1200	
Income		*Income*	*250*	

Year 8	$/mo. cap fund	Year 8	$/mo. cap fund	77175
Mo 1		Mo 1 (22%)	1415	6431
Mo 2		Mo 2	1415	6431
Mo 3		Mo 3	1415	6431
Mo 4		Mo 4	1415	6431
Mo 5		Mo 5	1415	6431
Mo 6		Mo 6	1415	6431
Mo 7		Mo 7	1415	6431
Mo 8		Mo 8	1415	6431
Mo 9		Mo 9	1415	6431
Mo10		Mo10	1415	6431
Mo11		Mo11	1415	6431
Mo12		Mo12	1415	6431
		Total	**16980**	**77172**
Purchase		Purchase	50000	
Property		Property	11, 12	
Down		Down	16000	
Payment		Payment	1000	
Income		*Income*	*300*	

Year 9	$/mo. cap fund	Year 9	$/mo. cap fund	81031
Mo 1		Mo 1 (25%)	1688	6753
Mo 2		Mo 2	1688	6753
Mo 3		Mo 3	1688	6753
Mo 4		Mo 4	1688	6753
Mo 5		Mo 5	1688	6753
Mo 6		Mo 6	1688	6753
Mo 7		Mo 7	1688	6753
Mo 8		Mo 8	1688	6753
Mo 9		Mo 9	1688	6753
Mo10		Mo10	1688	6753
Mo11		Mo11	1688	6753
Mo12		Mo12	1688	6753
		Total	**20256**	**81036**
Purchase		Purchase	75000 (2)	
Property		Property	13, 14	
Down		Down	20000	
Payment		Payment	1500	
Income		*Income*	*300*	

Year 10	$/mo. cap fund	Year 10	$/mo. cap fund	90000
Mo 1		Mo 1	1875	7500
Mo 2		Mo 2	1875	7500
Mo 3		Mo 3	1875	7500
Mo 4		Mo 4	1875	7500
Mo 5		Mo 5	1875	7500
Mo 6		Mo 6	1875	7500
Mo 7		Mo 7	1875	7500
Mo 8		Mo 8	1875	7500
Mo 9		Mo 9	1875	7500
Mo10		Mo10	1875	7500
Mo11		Mo11	1875	7500
Mo12		Mo12	1875	7500
		Total	**22500**	**90000**
Purchase		Purchase	50000 (2)	
Property		Property	15,16	
Down		Down	22000	
Payment		Payment	1000	
Income		*Income*	*300*	

Year 11	$/mo. cap fund	Year 11	$/mo. cap fund	94500
Mo 1		Mo 1	1968	7875
Mo 2		Mo 2	1968	7875
Mo 3		Mo 3	1968	7875
Mo 4		Mo 4	1968	7875
Mo 5		Mo 5	1968	7875
Mo 6		Mo 6	1968	7875
Mo 7		Mo 7	1968	7875
Mo 8		Mo 8	1968	7875
Mo 9		Mo 9	1968	7875
Mo10		Mo10	1968	7875
Mo11		Mo11	1968	7875
Mo12		Mo12	1968	7875
		Total	**23616**	**94500**
Purchase		Purchase	100000 (2)	
Property		Property	16, 17	
Down		Down	24000	
Payment		Payment	2500	
Income		*Income*	*500*	

Year 12	$/mo. cap fund	Year 12	$/mo. cap fund	99225
Mo 1		Mo 1	2067	8269
Mo 2		Mo 2	2067	8269
Mo 3		Mo 3	2067	8269
Mo 4		Mo 4	2067	8269
Mo 5		Mo 5	2067	8269
Mo 6		Mo 6	2067	8269
Mo 7		Mo 7	2067	8269
Mo 8		Mo 8	2067	8269
Mo 9		Mo 9	2067	8269
Mo10		Mo10	2067	8269
Mo11		Mo11	2067	8269
Mo12		Mo12	2067	8269
		Total	**24804**	**99228**
Purchase		Purchase	100000 (2)	
Property		Property	18, 19	
Down		Down	24000	
Payment		Payment	2500	
Income		*Income*	*500*	

Year 13	$/mo. cap fund	Year 13		$/mo. cap fund	104186
Mo 1		Mo 1		2171	8682
Mo 2		Mo 2		2171	8682
Mo 3		Mo 3		2171	8682
Mo 4		Mo 4		2171	8682
Mo 5		Mo 5		2171	8682
Mo 6		Mo 6		2171	8682
Mo 7		Mo 7		2171	8682
Mo 8		Mo 8		2171	8682
Mo 9		Mo 9		2171	8682
Mo10		Mo10		2171	8682
Mo11		Mo11		2171	8682
Mo12		Mo12		2171	8682
		Total		**26052**	**104184**
Purchase		Purchase	75000 (3)		
Property		Property	20, 21, 22		
Down		Down		27000	
Payment		Payment		2500	
Income		Income		600	

Year 14	$/mo. cap fund	Year 14		$/mo. cap fund	109393
Mo 1		Mo 1		2279	9116
Mo 2		Mo 2		2279	9116
Mo 3		Mo 3		2279	9116
Mo 4		Mo 4		2279	9116
Mo 5		Mo 5		2279	9116
Mo 6		Mo 6		2279	9116
Mo 7		Mo 7		2279	9116
Mo 8		Mo 8		2279	9116
Mo 9		Mo 9		2279	9116
Mo10		Mo10		2279	9116
Mo11		Mo11		2279	9116
Mo12		Mo12		2279	9116
		Total		**27348**	**109392**
Purchase		Purchase	100000 (2)		
Property		Property	23, 24		
Down		Down		25000	
Payment		Payment		2500	
Income		Income		500	

Year 15	$/mo. cap fund	Year 15	$/mo. cap fund	125000

Mo 1	Mo 1	2604	10417
Mo 2	Mo 2	2604	10417
Mo 3	Mo 3	2604	10417
Mo 4	Mo 4	2604	10417
Mo 5	Mo 5	2604	10417
Mo 6	Mo 6	2604	10417
Mo 7	Mo 7	2604	10417
Mo 8	Mo 8	2604	10417
Mo 9	Mo 9	2604	10417
Mo10	Mo10	2604	10417
Mo11	Mo11	2604	10417
Mo12	Mo12	2604	10417
	Total	**31248**	**125004**
Purchase	Purchase	75000 (3)	
Property	Property	25, 26, 27	
Down	Down	30000	
Payment	Payment	2500	
Income	*Income*	*750*	

Year 16	$/mo. cap fund	Year 16	$/mo. cap fund	137000
Mo 1		Mo 1	2854	11417
Mo 2		Mo 2	2854	11417
Mo 3		Mo 3	2854	11417
Mo 4		Mo 4	2854	11417
Mo 5		Mo 5	2854	11417
Mo 6		Mo 6	2854	11417
Mo 7		Mo 7	2854	11417
Mo 8		Mo 8	2854	11417
Mo 9		Mo 9	2854	11417
Mo10		Mo10	2854	11417
Mo11		Mo11	2854	11417
Mo12		Mo12	2854	11417
		Total	**34248**	**137004**
Purchase		Purchase	100000 (3)	
Property		Property	28, 29, 30	
Down		Down	35000	
Payment		Payment	3500	
Income		*Income*	*1000*	

Year 17	$/mo. cap fund	Year 17	$/mo. cap fund	150000+

Mo 1	Mo 1	3125	12500
Mo 2	Mo 2	3125	12500
Mo 3	Mo 3	3125	12500
Mo 4	Mo 4	3125	12500
Mo 5	Mo 5	3125	12500
Mo 6	Mo 6	3125	12500
Mo 7	Mo 7	3125	12500
Mo 8	Mo 8	3125	12500
Mo 9	Mo 9	3125	12500
Mo10	Mo10	3125	12500
Mo11	Mo11	3125	12500
Mo12	Mo12	3125	12500
	Total	**37500**	**150000**

Purchase

Property   Loan Reduct.37000

Down

Payment

Income

Year 18	$/mo. cap fund	Year 18	$/mo. cap fund	160000+
Mo 1		Mo 1	3333	13333
Mo 2		Mo 2	3333	13333
Mo 3		Mo 3	3333	13333
Mo 4		Mo 4	3333	13333
Mo 5		Mo 5	3333	13333
Mo 6		Mo 6	3333	13333
Mo 7		Mo 7	3333	13333
Mo 8		Mo 8	3333	13333
Mo 9		Mo 9	3333	13333
Mo10		Mo10	3333	13333
Mo11		Mo11	3333	13333
Mo12		Mo12	3333	13333
		Total	**39996**	**159996**

Purchase

Property   Loan Reduce   40000

Down

Payment

Income

Year 19 $/mo. cap fund   Year 19 $/mo. cap fund   175000+

Mo 1	Mo 1	3645	14583
Mo 2	Mo 2	3645	14583
Mo 3	Mo 3	3645	14583
Mo 4	Mo 4	3645	14583
Mo 5	Mo 5	3645	14583
Mo 6	Mo 6	3645	14583
Mo 7	Mo 7	3645	14583
Mo 8	Mo 8	3645	14583
Mo 9	Mo 9	3645	14583
Mo10	Mo10	3645	14583
Mo11	Mo11	3645	14583
Mo12	Mo12	3645	14583
	Total	**43740**	**174996**
Purchase			
Property	Loan Reduce	43500	
Down			
Payment			
Income			

Year 20 $/mo. cap fund	Year 20 $/mo. cap fund		175000
Mo 1	Mo 1	3645	14583
Mo 2	Mo 2	3645	14583
Mo 3	Mo 3	3645	14583
Mo 4	Mo 4	3645	14583
Mo 5	Mo 5	3645	14583
Mo 6	Mo 6	3645	14583
Mo 7	Mo 7	3645	14583
Mo 8	Mo 8	3645	14583
Mo 9	Mo 9	3645	14583
Mo10	Mo10	3645	14583
Mo11	Mo11	3645	14583
Mo12	Mo12	3645	14583
	Total	**43740**	**174996**
Purchase			
Property	Loan Reduce	43500	
Down			
Payment			
Income			

Year 21 $/mo. cap fund	Year 21 $/mo. cap fund		200000

Mo 1	Mo 1	4167	16667
Mo 2	Mo 2	4167	16667
Mo 3	Mo 3	4167	16667
Mo 4	Mo 4	4167	16667
Mo 5	Mo 5	4167	16667
Mo 6	Mo 6	4167	16667
Mo 7	Mo 7	4167	16667
Mo 8	Mo 8	4167	16667
Mo 9	Mo 9	4167	16667
Mo10	Mo10	4167	16667
Mo11	Mo11	4167	16667
Mo12	Mo12	4167	16667
	Total	**50004**	**200004**

Purchase

Property   Loan Reduce   50000

Down

Payment

Income

Year 22 $/mo. cap fund	Year 22 $/mo. cap fund		200000
Mo 1	Mo 1	4167	16667
Mo 2	Mo 2	4167	16667
Mo 3	Mo 3	4167	16667
Mo 4	Mo 4	4167	16667
Mo 5	Mo 5	4167	16667
Mo 6	Mo 6	4167	16667
Mo 7	Mo 7	4167	16667
Mo 8	Mo 8	4167	16667
Mo 9	Mo 9	4167	16667
Mo10	Mo10	4167	16667
Mo11	Mo11	4167	16667
Mo12	Mo12	4167	16667
	Total	**50004**	**200004**

Purchase

Property   Loan Reduce   50000

Down

Payment

Income

Year 23 $/mo. cap fund   Year 23 $/mo. cap fund   225000

Mo 1	Mo 1	4688	18750
Mo 2	Mo 2	4688	18750
Mo 3	Mo 3	4688	18750
Mo 4	Mo 4	4688	18750
Mo 5	Mo 5	4688	18750
Mo 6	Mo 6	4688	18750
Mo 7	Mo 7	4688	18750
Mo 8	Mo 8	4688	18750
Mo 9	Mo 9	4688	18750
Mo10	Mo10	4688	18750
Mo11	Mo11	4688	18750
Mo12	Mo12	4688	18750
	Total	**56256**	**225000**

Purchase

Property   Loan Reduce   56000

Down

Payment

Income

Year 24	$/mo. cap fund	Year 24	$/mo. cap fund	250000
Mo 1		Mo 1	5208	20833
Mo 2		Mo 2	5208	20833
Mo 3		Mo 3	5208	20833
Mo 4		Mo 4	5208	20833
Mo 5		Mo 5	5208	20833
Mo 6		Mo 6	5208	20833
Mo 7		Mo 7	5208	20833
Mo 8		Mo 8	5208	20833
Mo 9		Mo 9	5208	20833
Mo10		Mo10	5208	20833
Mo11		Mo11	5208	20833
Mo12		Mo12	5208	20833
		Total	**62496**	**249996**

Purchase

Property   Loan Reduce   62500

Down

Payment

Income

Year 25	$/mo. cap fund	Year 25	$/mo. cap fund	25000

Mo 1	Mo 1	5208	20833
Mo 2	Mo 2	5208	20833
Mo 3	Mo 3	5208	20833
Mo 4	Mo 4	5208	20833
Mo 5	Mo 5	5208	20833
Mo 6	Mo 6	5208	20833
Mo 7	Mo 7	5208	20833
Mo 8	Mo 8	5208	20833
Mo 9	Mo 9	5208	20833
Mo10	Mo10	5208	20833
Mo11	Mo11	5208	20833
Mo12	Mo12	5208	20833
	Total	**62496**	**249996**

Purchase

Property

Loan
Reduce 62500

Down
Payment
Income

Coach Dr. JAG

Look for other Coach Dr JAG books on business, investing, Business skills, and leadership at your favorite book seller.

Check out www.lifemapsonline.net for additional resources available.

Visit website for the current free offer when you contact LifeMAPS Consulting or Coach Dr. JAG at www.lifemapsonline.net.

Get a free book when you register as a visitor.

Resources:

Coach Dr JAG Books

Look for other Coach Dr JAG books that offer insights in the following areas in 2016 and 2017. Coach Dr. JAG books are intended to provide general information on key topics for improved business, investing, and quality of life skills.

Investing in Wealth: Journey of a Penny to Wealth
Success in Social Networking
The Leader Relationship
WAH Factor and Other Lame Excuses
Foundations in Coaching
Core 4 Life Management